DATE DUE

A guided trip through the national parks in Montana, Wyoming, and South Dakota. Here are glaciers and mountains, lakes and waterfalls, hot springs and geysers, and all the wonders of Glacier, Yellowstone, and Grand Teton. Interesting descriptions and beautiful color photographs.

OUR NATIONAL PARKS

Yellowstone
Glacier
Grand Teton

by Frances Wood

Illustrated with photographs in color

FOLLETT PUBLISHING COMPANY   CHICAGO

123456789

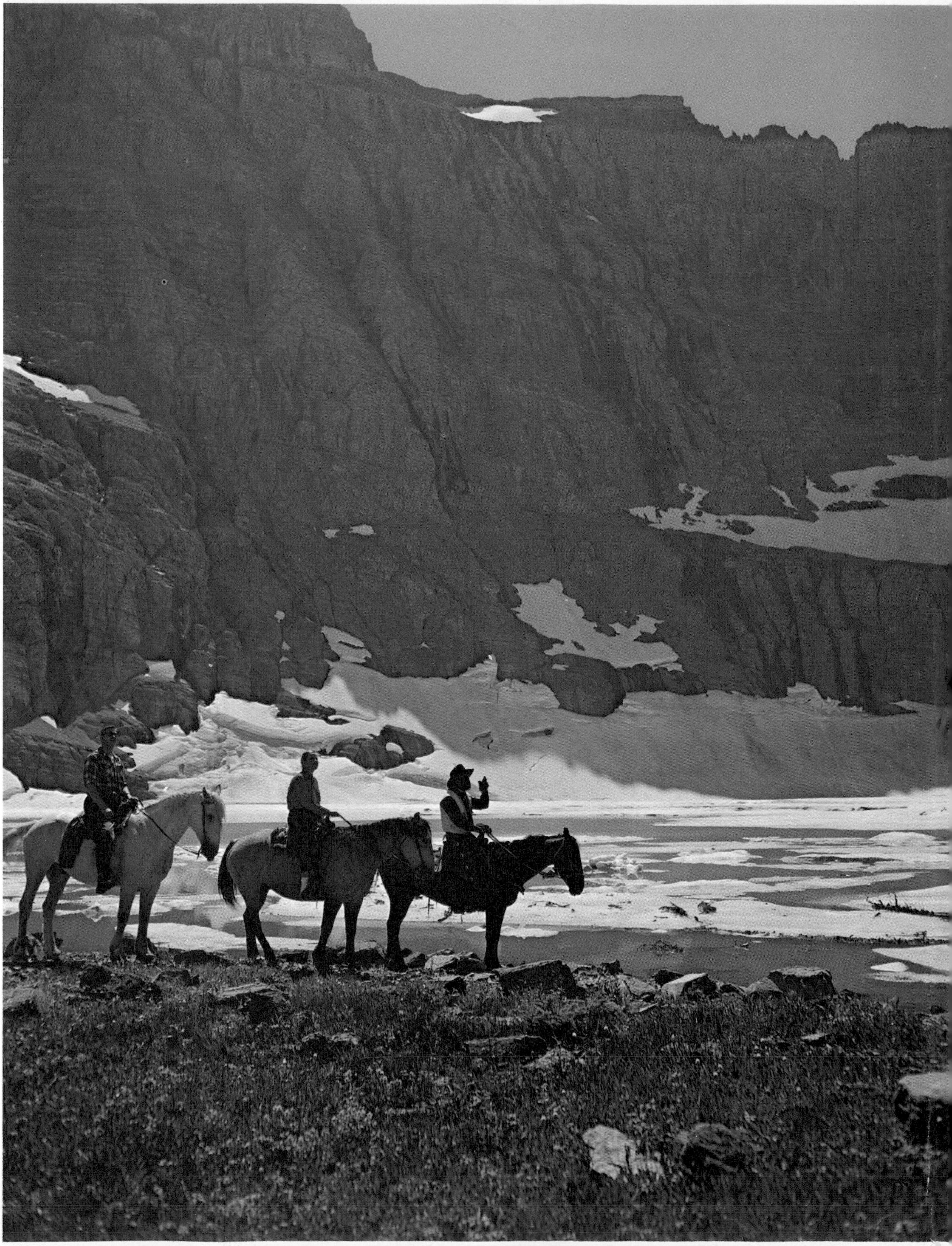
Great Northern Railway

Lake McDonald Hotel, on the shore of Glacier Park's largest lake, welcomes visitors entering from the west.

Our National Parks

Our national parks and monuments preserve areas of outstanding scenic and scientific interest for everyone to see and enjoy. Yellowstone, established by Congress in 1872, was the first of the national parks. Today there are thirty-one national parks, covering a total area of 13,000,000 miles. Twenty-two million persons visit the national parks each year.

The National Park Service builds roads and trails and campgrounds in the parks. It constructs museums, visitor centers, and other buildings.

The park rangers watch out for the safety and comfort of the visitors. And they do many things to help us understand and enjoy the parks. They set up exhibits, lead nature walks, give lectures, and hold campfire meetings.

The rangers also enforce park rules and protect the wildlife in the park.

3

A guide and visitors at Iceberg Lake near Many Glacier Hotel in Glacier National Park.

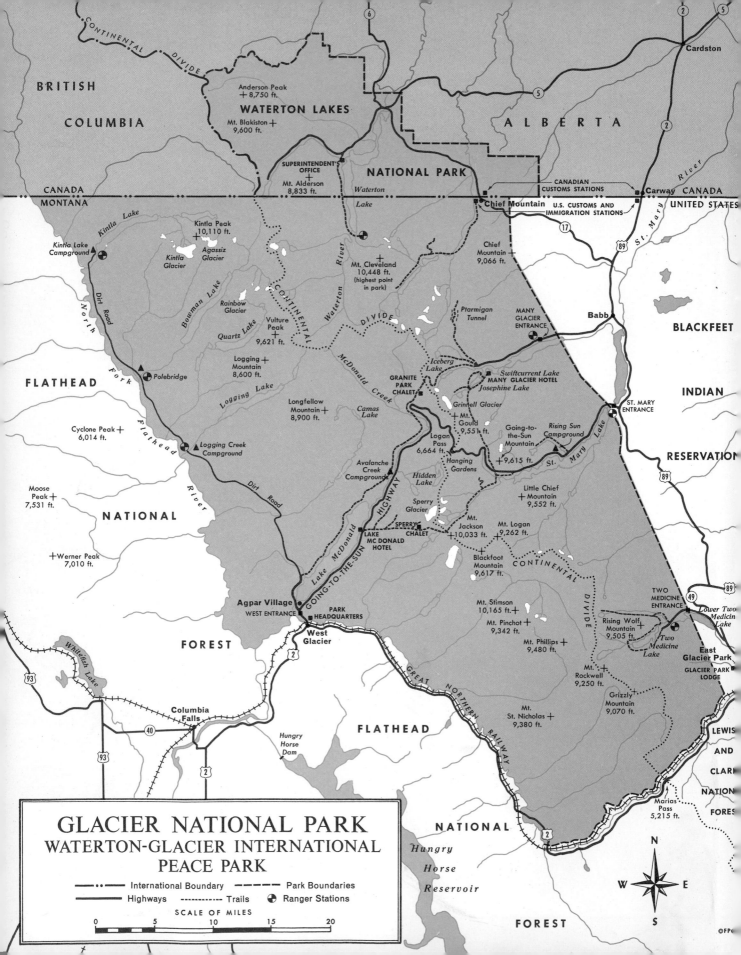

GLACIER NATIONAL PARK
WATERTON-GLACIER INTERNATIONAL PEACE PARK

International Boundary   Park Boundaries
Highways   Trails   Ranger Stations

SCALE OF MILES
0   5   10   15   20

Great Northern Railway

The mountains of Glacier National Park as seen from Logan Pass. The animal in the foreground is a marmot.

Glacier National Park

This park, with its glaciers, snow-capped peaks, and sparkling lakes, lies in northern Montana. The Continental Divide, which follows the highest mountain ranges on the North American continent, goes through the middle of the park.

The Divide runs diagonally from central Alaska in the north through Central America in the south. In the United States, most streams east of the Divide flow into the Mississippi River. Those on the west flow into the Pacific Ocean.

Glacier Park joins Canada's Waterton National Park, and the two parks are called the Waterton-Glacier International Peace Park.

A ranger guides a nature walk on Grinnell Glacier near Many Glacier Hotel.

Much of the park's rugged beauty is due to the work of glaciers. These are formed where the weather is so cold that the snow never melts. Finally it is pressed into ice sheets by its own weight.

Thousands of years ago the whole area was covered by great ice sheets. Only the highest peaks rose above the ice. The valleys were filled with slowly moving glaciers that carried rocks and gravel and sand along with them. These glaciers scraped out the bottoms of the valleys and made them U-shaped.

Sometimes a glacier scooped out a round place in the mountain at the head of the valley. These places are called "cirques." Often they contain lovely little lakes almost surrounded by cliffs.

The park contains about 60 small glaciers. None of them are near the road, but several can be reached by trails. The largest are Sperry and Grinnell glaciers, and

Iceberg Lake is a good example of a lake in a cirque. This picture is of a small lake below Iceberg Lake, known as Little Iceberg Lake. It is in the same cirque as Iceberg Lake, and the headwall behind it encompasses Iceberg Lake too.

park naturalists lead tours to each of these.

Some peaks have been deeply carved on all sides by glaciers, making them sharp and thin. These peaks are called "horns." Other mountains have been sliced into thin, jagged walls. The Garden Wall is one of these.

One of the first things we notice when we enter the park are the striking colors in the mountains— light green, red, buff, black, and white. The black band in the Garden Wall is shown below.

Waterfalls are everywhere. They flow over benches of rock and drop down the sides of mountains. When the ice melts, they form sparkling cascades down the glacier walls.

Mount Gould, reflected in the waters of Lake Josephine. The black band in the Garden wall can be seen in the background.

Great Northern Railway

7

Chief Mountain.

Several short roads go to the large lakes on the east side of the park, and the Going-to-the-Sun Road crosses it from east to west. But Glacier is principally a trails park. There are fewer than 100 miles of roads and more than 1,000 miles of trails.

On the east, the Blackfeet Highway goes north to Canada, and a side road from it cuts across the corner of the park, past Chief Mountain, to Waterton Park. The Theodore Roosevelt Highway follows the park's southern boundary.

A bull moose.

Going-to-the-Sun Mountain at sunrise.

A narrow dirt road goes north from Lake McDonald to Bowman and Kintla lakes, with trails to Logging and Quartz lakes. Moose can often be seen along this road, and fishing is good in the lakes.

There is something to be seen along every mile of magnificent Going-to-the-Sun Road. Interesting animals, towering mountains, wildflowers, waterfalls, St. Mary Lake are some of the sights.

The road crosses the Continental Divide at Logan Pass. It has been climbing up the east side of the mountains. At this point it starts down the west side.

A wide parking area at the Pass allows visitors to leave their cars and look around. Near the parking area is a deposit of fossil plants that grew here millions of years ago when the area was covered by water. A short trail goes to a broad meadow of flowers, called the Hanging Gardens. Another trail leads to a fine view of Hidden Lake.

Going-to-the-Sun Highway, following St. Mary Lake.

Weeping Wall.

Below Logan Pass the road goes north, along the west side of the Garden Wall, where it sometimes runs between banks of snow. Weeping Wall, from which water drips continually, extends for several hundred feet along the road. A trail above the road goes to Granite Park Chalets, where hikers and riders can get overnight accommodations.

After leaving the Garden Wall, the road makes a great loop south and follows McDonald Creek to Lake McDonald, largest in the park. There are good accommodations here, free campgrounds, and boat trips on the lake. A trail goes to Sperry Glacier by way of Sperry Chalets.

There is always something to do at the lakes on the east side of the park—fishing, hiking, horseback riding, boat trips, and campfires in the evening.

At Swiftcurrent Lake, in the Many Glacier area, there are campgrounds, cottages, and a large hotel. From nearby Josephine Lake is a splendid view of Grinnell Glacier and the east side of the Garden Wall. Grinnell Lake and the glacier can be reached by good trails.

Beargrass at Swiftcurrent Lake. In the background is snow-draped Mount Wilbur.

Josef Muench

Great Northern Railway

Indians at their camp near hotel at East Glacier.

A six-mile trail goes to Iceberg Lake, where icebergs float most of the summer. This is a good example of a lake in a cirque, almost surrounded by cliffs. Beargrass and other flowers grow thick along the trail.

East Glacier, just outside the park, is on the edge of the Blackfeet Indian Reservation, and the Indians come to town in their attractive native dress. In the evenings they hold tribal dances at Glacier Park Lodge. A few miles away, at Browning, a fine museum and crafts center tell the story of the Plains Indians.

Beautiful Two Medicine Lake is reached by a short road from East Glacier. About 400 yards off this road, famous Trick Falls attract many sightseers. At first glance, there appears to be just one waterfall. But a second look will detect a second waterfall coming out of a tunnel about a third of the way from the bottom.

Trick Falls, on the way to Two Medicine Lake.

12

The ptarmigan, or grouse, an interesting bird that turns white in winter, may often be seen on Logan Pass and around Iceberg Lake. A small gray bird called the water ouzel dives into rushing mountain streams and walks along the bottom, looking for food. It often nests behind waterfalls.

Mountain goats on a steep cliffside.

Many kinds of animals live in the park. Mountain goats and bighorn sheep inhabit the peaks. They can be seen from several points on Going-to-the-Sun Road and from many spots along the trails. Elk, deer, moose, and bear often appear in McDonald Valley and elsewhere.

Squirrels, marmots, and friendly chipmunks play among the rocks. Pikas, which look somewhat like tiny rabbits, scurry about, harvesting grass and other plants for their winter food supply.

A friendly Columbian ground squirrel holds a cherry given him by a visitor.

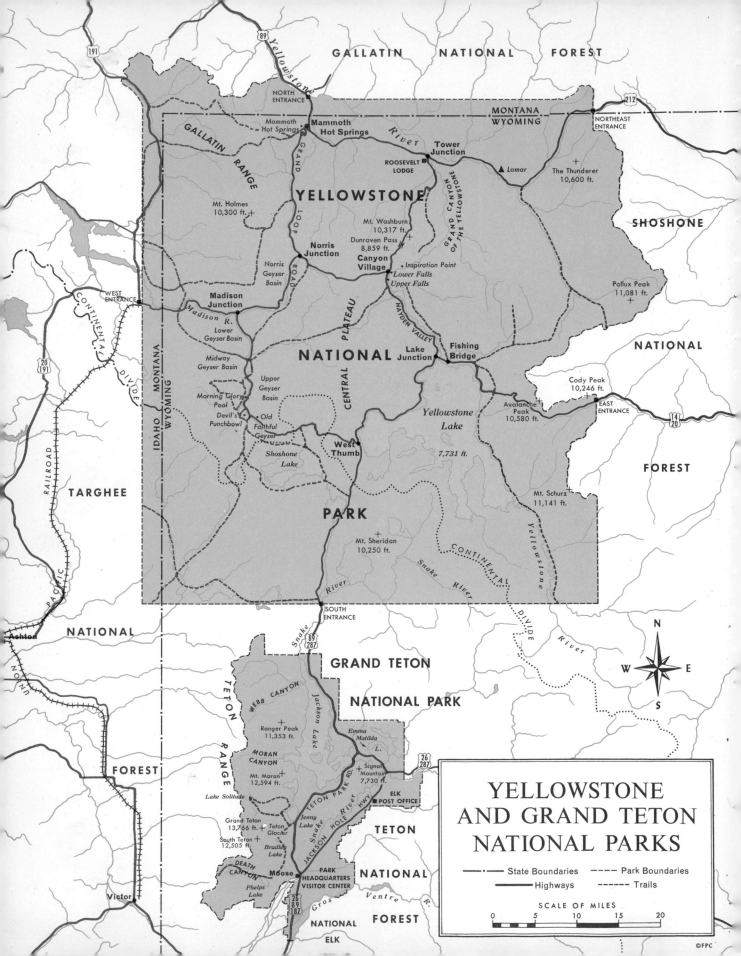

GALLATIN   NATIONAL   FOREST

89
191

Yellowstone

NORTH
ENTRANCE

Mammoth
Hot Springs
Mammoth Hot Springs

212

River

MONTANA
WYOMING

NORTHEAST
ENTRANCE

GALLATIN RANGE

Tower
Junction

ROOSEVELT
LODGE

▲ Lamar

The Thunderer
10,600 ft.

SHOSHONE

YELLOWSTONE

Mt. Holmes
10,300 ft. +

Norris
Junction

Mt. Washburn
10,317 ft. +
Dunraven Pass
8,859 ft.

Canyon
Village

GRAND CANYON OF THE YELLOWSTONE

Pollux Peak
11,081 ft.
+

GRAND LOOP ROAD

Norris
Geyser
Basin

• Inspiration Point
Lower Falls
Upper Falls

WEST
ENTRANCE

CONTINENTAL DIVIDE

Madison
Junction

Madison R.
Lower
Geyser Basin

NATIONAL

Lake
Junction

Fishing
Bridge

HAYDEN VALLEY

NATIONAL

20
191

Midway
Geyser Basin

CENTRAL PLATEAU

Cody Peak
10,246 ft.

EAST
ENTRANCE

14
20

IDAHO MONTANA
WYOMING

Upper
Geyser
Basin

Morning Glory
Pool
Devil's
Punchbowl

Old
Faithful
Geyser

Yellowstone
Lake

Avalanche
Peak
10,580 ft.

FOREST

West
Thumb

7,731 ft.

Shoshone
Lake

RAILROAD

TARGHEE

PARK

Mt. Schurz
11,141 ft.
+

Mt. Sheridan
10,250 ft. +

CONTINENTAL

Yellowstone

PACIFIC

Snake
River

Snake River

DIVIDE

River

SOUTH
ENTRANCE

N

Ashton

NATIONAL

89
287

GRAND TETON

W   E

UNION

NATIONAL PARK

S

WEBB CANYON

Jackson Lake

Ranger Peak
11,353 ft.

Emma
Matilda
L.

FOREST

TETON RANGE

MORAN
CANYON

Mt. Moran
12,594 ft.

Signal
Mountain
7,730 ft.

26
287

Lake Solitude

TETON PARK RD.

ELK
POST OFFICE

Grand Teton
13,766 ft. +
Teton
Glacier
South Teton
12,505 ft. +

Jenny
Lake

Bradley
Lake

Snake River

JACKSON HOLE HWY.

TETON

YELLOWSTONE
AND GRAND TETON
NATIONAL PARKS

DEATH
CANYON

Moose

PARK
HEADQUARTERS
VISITOR CENTER

NATIONAL

—·—·— State Boundaries   — — — Park Boundaries

Victor

Phelps
Lake

26
89
187

Gros

Ventre

R.

FOREST

———— Highways   - - - - Trails

SCALE OF MILES

0   5   10   15   20

NATIONAL
ELK

©FPC

Norris Geyser Basin.

Yellowstone National Park

Yellowstone, which spills across the northwest corner of Wyoming into Idaho and Montana, is a land of wonders. Steam rises from thousands of colorful hot springs and pools. Two hundred geysers send columns of water into the air.

Mud volcanoes bubble and boil. Paint pots contain brightly colored mud that looks like boiling paint.

Grand Prismatic Spring, in Midway Geyser Basin, is the largest hot spring in the basin.

Yellowstone is a land of change, too. Pools and geysers dry up, and new geysers blow off.

Many changes occurred in the summer of 1959, when a severe earthquake shook the area. Just outside the park, the whole side of a mountain fell into the Madison River. This formed a dam and made a new lake, Earthquake Lake.

Inside the park, famous Grand Geyser stopped erupting, and Turquoise Spring dried up. New geysers began erupting, and new paint pots were formed. Lovely Sapphire Pool became a geyser.

16

At one time there were many volcanoes in the Yellowstone area, and layers of rock beneath the earth are still hot. Water that seeps down through cracks in the rock is heated and returns to the surface as hot springs and pools.

A geyser is formed when the water seeps from the cracks into a channel, like a tube, running down through very hard rock. The water at the bottom of the tube gets hotter and hotter until it is turned into steam. The steam pushes up harder and harder against the water above it.

Finally, so much steam forms and the pressure becomes so great that water and steam blow high into the air. The eruption lasts until most of the water in the geyser tube has been forced out.

The Devil's Punch Bowl, in Black Sands Basin.

Union Pacific Railroad

Old Faithful Geyser, in the Upper Basin near famous Old Faithful Inn, erupts on an average of every 65 minutes. The eruption lasts for about four minutes.

Old Faithful was given its name in 1869, when the Yellowstone area was explored by the Washburn-Langford expedition. It has been erupting regularly ever since, sending a leaping column of steaming water to heights of 115 to 150 feet and sometimes higher. Giant Geyser sends its water as high as 250 feet, but it does not erupt regularly.

Morning Glory Pool, also in the Upper Basin, is almost as popular as Old Faithful. The Devil's Punch Bowl, in nearby Black Sands Basin, is another outstanding sight.

Lovely Morning Glory Pool is named for its flowerlike cone.

Across the deep blue of Yellowstone Lake are seen the snow-capped mountains that feed it.

East of Old Faithful, across the mountains, is Yellowstone Lake, the largest and most beautiful lake in the park. It is about 20 miles long and 15 miles wide, with 100 miles of shoreline. The lake is shaped somewhat like a hand with the fingers spread. For a panoramic view of the lake, visitors may follow the road eastward 10 miles to Lake Butte. Yellowstone Lake is fed by snow from the mountains that surround most of it. The water is clear and cold. This is the largest lake in North America at such a high elevation—7,731 feet above sea level.

Yellowstone Lake is famous not only for its beauty, but for the fighting cutthroat, or blackspotted, trout that make it a popular fishing area. People fish along the shore and from boats.

The Grand Loop Road goes along the west shore of the lake, past hot springs and paint pots and geysers, to Fishing Bridge. This bridge, across Yellowstone River at the outlet of the lake, is usually lined with fishermen from dawn to dusk.

From Fishing Bridge, the road follows a scenic course along the Yellowstone River. In Hayden Valley, buffalo can sometimes be seen feeding near the highway.

On the route through Hayden Valley, the road passes the Mud Volcano area. Not far away by trail is the Black Dragons Caldron.

The famous Fishing Bridge at the outlet of Yellowstone Lake.

Another outstanding attraction is the Grand Canyon of the Yellowstone River and its magnificent Upper and Lower Falls. The Lower, or Great Falls, twice as high as Niagara, drop with a mighty roar more than 300 feet into the canyon below. Often the spray at the bottom of the falls is beautifully tinted with rainbow colors.

The steep, rugged walls of the canyon are lined with yellow rock, shading into orange and pink and red. That is why the river and park were named Yellowstone.

Near Canyon Village, side roads lead to Artist Point, Lookout Point, Inspiration Point, Grandview Point and others from which spectacular views of the canyon and the falls can be seen.

Mammoth Hot Springs was named for the large springs in the area. The hot water in the springs contains a white mineral called lime. When the water flows over the sides of the springs, the lime builds up basins, or terraces, around each spring. Many of these terraces are beautifully colored by tiny plants which grow in the water.

There are overnight accommodations and campgrounds at Mammoth Hot Springs and other points on the Grand Loop Road.

The terraces at Mammoth Hot Springs.

James Simon

23

Mother bear and cub at Yellowstone.

Evergreen forests cover much of Yellowstone, and flowers carpet many of the valleys and meadows.

Bears are often seen along the road. They should be observed only at a safe distance, and park rules forbid feeding them. Antelopes graze in the area west of Mammoth Hot Springs. Deer and elk visit the geyser basins. Other animals are buffalo, moose, coyote, and bighorn sheep. Many of these stay in the wilderness, reached only by trails.

There are many waterfowl and other birds in the park. Geese and ducks visit the lakes in large numbers. Gulls, pelicans, and ospreys, or fish hawks, are at Yellowstone Lake. Eagles nest among the high crags.

Pronghorn antelope.

Trumpeter swan.

Pelicans.

Grand Teton National Park

This park, south of Yellowstone, contains one of the most beautiful mountain ranges in the world—the Tetons. At the foot of the range lies a wide, lake-studded valley, known as Jackson Hole. The Snake River flows through it.

Unlike most mountains, the Tetons do not have foothills with gently sloping sides. Instead, these mountains rise straight upward from the valley floor and thrust their sharp and jagged peaks toward the sky.

Glaciers like those in Glacier National Park carved the sharp peaks and scooped out valleys and lakes. A few small glaciers still lie among the mountain peaks. Streams cut deep canyons as they flowed down the steep sides of the mountains.

The Snake River and the Grand Teton Range.

Union Pacific Railroad

The grandeur of the Tetons as seen across Jenny Lake.

Much activity centers around Jackson and Jenny lakes. There is water skiing on Jackson Lake, largest in the park, and a boat trip goes all around it. Visitors who are there on a moonlit night can go on a picnic cruise and have a campfire supper on an island in the lake.

There are boat trips on Jenny Lake and fine fishing here and in nearby lakes. Both Jenny and Jackson lakes have good overnight accommodations, free campgrounds, and interesting museums.

It is fun to take a float trip down the Snake River from Jackson Lake to Moose. At Moose is the lovely little Chapel of the Transfiguration, and people come from miles around to attend church in it.

Historic Menors Ferry has been restored to look just as it did when it was used in the early days to cross the Snake River.

A good highway leads south through the park past Jackson and Jenny lakes and Moose. Another highway goes from Jackson Lake Lodge to the Wildlife Range, where we can see elk and buffalo. North of the Range are the Emma Matilda and Two Ocean lakes. A surfaced road goes up Signal Mountain for a fine view of the Teton Range and Jackson Hole, with its string of lakes.

Flower-lined trails go from Jenny Lake to nearby lakes. Longer, steeper trails lead to mountains and canyons in the wilderness areas. Hidden Falls, near the west shore of Jenny Lake, can be reached by boat and trail or by a longer trail around the lake.

Trout are plentiful in the swift rivers, lakes, and ponds of Jackson Hole, and fishing is a favorite sport in the park. The rocky summits of Mount Moran, Grand Teton, Teewinot, and other mountains of the Teton Range challenge skilled climbers.

Horseback riding over the winding trails is another favorite activity. Pack trips, with guides to make camp and cook the meals over a campfire, are popular.

The Church of the Transfiguration.

Cooking out at Jackson Hole.

Mabel Siders

Josef Muench

A fine mule deer buck in his winter coat, with the velvet gone from his big antlers.

Jackson Hole is famous for its big-game animals. Moose feed along the edges of ponds and marshes. Huge herds of elk winter in the Hole and move up to higher country in the summer. Mule deer sometimes forage near the road.

Beavers build their dams in many of the streams, and marmots whistle at us from the rocks. Pikas harvest their crops and spread them out to dry.

Two friendly little animals that look alike are the golden-mantled ground squirrel and the chipmunk. But the squirrel is larger, and his stripes stop at his shoulders, while those of the chipmunk run to the end of his nose.

Waterfowl that visit the park include wild geese and ducks, great blue herons, and the rare trumpeter swan. The swans are shy, however, and try to keep out of sight.

Golden-mantled ground squirrel.

James Simon

Elk in winter at Jackson Hole.   Union Pacific Railroad

Chipmunk.   James Simon

Great blue heron.

James Simon   *Prairie dogs.*

Devil's Tower National Monument

In the northeastern corner of Wyoming is Devil's Tower, our first national monument. It is a great tower of fluted rock that rises 865 feet from the ridge at its base. It was probably formed by a volcanic eruption long, long ago.

At the base of the Tower are picnic and campgrounds and a prairie-dog town.

Devil's Tower.

Wyoming Highway Dept.

29

The face of George Washington was the first to be completed. The sculpture was begun in 1927 and the fourth likeness, that of Theodore Roosevelt, was finished in 1941.

South Dakota Dept. of Hys.

Mount Rushmore National Memorial

The Black Hills of South Dakota are a delightful vacationland for millions of people each year. The mountains are the highest east of the Rockies. Because of the elevation the area provides cool, restful nights. Harney Peak in the Black Hills is 7,242 feet high. From the Ranger Station at its top, four states can be seen.

An outstanding attraction for visitors to the Black Hills is Mount Rushmore National Memorial. On the face of a granite cliff 6,040 feet high are the likenesses of four of our greatest presidents. The faces of George Washington, Thomas Jefferson, Theodore Roosevelt, and Abraham Lincoln were carved by Gutzon Borglum, a noted sculptor. The faces are about 60 feet tall and can be seen from 60 miles away. Lighted by floodlights after dark, the memorial is an inspiring sight against the night sky.

30

A bridge on the road to Mt. Rushmore. It is called a pigtail bridge because it curls up over itself.

A chamber over 200 feet below the surface in Wind Cave.

Wind Cave National Park

Wind Cave National Park, on the southeast flank of the Black Hills, preserves a beautiful little cave. On its walls and ceiling is an unusual formation that looks like fine lace. This is called boxwork. There are other formations, too.

Wind Cave got its name from the strange whistling sounds that wind currents make at the mouth of the cave.

Large buffalo herds roam the miles of prairie in this park and nearby Custer State Park. They can often be seen from the road.

Antelope, deer, elk, and many small animals also make their homes in the park. Several prairie-dog towns are near the road.

A buffalo herd on the prairie in Wind Cave National Park.

The Badlands of South Dakota.

Badlands National Monument

The Badlands National Monument is an area of highly colored peaks, buttes, ridges, and spires. The bones of many prehistoric animals, such as the sabre-toothed tiger and the three-toed horse have been found in the Badlands. Some of these skeletons can be seen on display in the South Dakota School of Mines Museum at Rapid City.

Every year thousands of people on western vacations pass through this part of South Dakota. As they drive along the road they stop at parking overlooks for a fine view of the bizarre pinnacles and knobs, the steep gullies and canyons, and all the varied formations. The strangely beautiful Badlands offer vacationers a fascinating introduction to the wonders of our western national parks.